Extolling Yeshua

Extolling Yeshua

JAMES S. ANDERSON

WIPF & STOCK · Eugene, Oregon

Wipf & Stock
An Imprint of Wipf and Stock Publishers
199 W. 8th Ave., Suite 3
Eugene, OR 97401

www.wipfandstock.com

PAPERBACK ISBN: 978-1-5326-7925-4
HARDCOVER ISBN: 978-1-5326-7926-1
EBOOK ISBN: 978-1-5326-7927-8

Manufactured in the U.S.A.   FEBRUARY 15, 2019

For my maker,
Though I am not always faithful,
I am ever so grateful you always are.

Contents

Illustrations

Introduction

THE INADEQUACY OF HUMAN words to give a true account of the word led St. Thomas Aquinas to conclude that "Everything which I have written seems like straw to me compared to what I have seen and what has been revealed to me." After that, Aquinas is said to have quit writing altogether.[1]

As much as Aquinas built his own work upon previous theological and philosophical treatises, the evangelists drew on a multitude of well-known figures from the Hebrew Scriptures as well as from ancient Near Eastern motifs to transmit as best as they could their understanding of this first-century rabbi who traversed Palestine with a message of redemption and love.

Yet, the Gospels are not merely imitating old models. In the sense that they used these models as a canvas for the Gospels, the theologians who wrote the New Testament deserve the title of "authors." Most of them, however, complied with the intellectual tradition of their days by not signing their work as modern authors are expected to do. Paul's letters are different. By definition, letters specify their author and sender. By contrast, the Gospels are not epistles.

1. See Caputo, *Heidegger and Aquinas*, 252–53.

They follow the ancient scribal practice of pseudepigraphy, i.e., the attribution of a literary work to a figure of the past, in the case of the Gospels, one of the twelve disciples (Matthew and John) or a follower of Peter (Mark). The actual writers used pseudonyms to avoid putting themselves forward as authors, leaving the narrative stage for their Lord. Such a self-effacing strategy provides access to the hero of the Gospels, an access mediated through older biblical and nonbiblical models rather than through an omniscient narrator, whose position would usurp God's place. Therefore, the evangelists will be referred to as writers rather than as authors throughout the present work.

After two millennia, the figures and motifs upon which the Gospel writers drew are not as readily apparent to modern readers of the New Testament as they were to the first generations of Christians. Ancient Near Eastern religions faded away with the advent of Christianity. In theory, the figures of the Old Testament fared better. The Old Testament, in its Greek version, was *the* Bible for the evangelists, but Christians tend, naturally enough, to be less acquainted with the Old Testament than with the New. Therefore, modern Bible readers miss out on much of the warp as much as the weft of the canvas upon which the Gospels created their account of Yeshua's ministry.

To differentiate the way Jesus is understood today from the way he was understood by his contemporaries, and even more so by the Gospel writers and their audience, the Aramaic form of Jesus' name, Yeshua, is used throughout the present work. With the encounter of the name by which the early Christians referred to Jesus, the reader is somewhat drawn into the ancient context in which Christianity was born. The Greek form *Iesous* would have been appropriate too, since the four canonical Gospels are written in Greek, but it is probably not how the disciples referred to their master since it is unlikely that Yeshua or any of his disciples were proficient in Greek.

That Yeshua was painted with recourse to well-known motifs in circulation at the time in no way diminishes our understanding of him. On the contrary, patterning Yeshua on figures of the past supplied a plethora of explanations in order to express who he was, extolling him in such a manner as to convey that he possessed those positive features of the giants of the past. Indeed, the appropriation and application of multiple motifs and patterns from the Old Testament for the portrayal of Yeshua in the New Testament allowed the Gospels to show that Yeshua surpasses any single person used to describe him, thus extolling him as one who is second to none.

What one often finds in the Gospels is the appropriation of Hebrew Bible figures and their mighty deeds applied to Yeshua. For example, Moses delivers the Israelites from bondage, Yeshua delivers humanity from bondage. On the broader scene of the Ancient Orient, the co-opting of the divine battle with the sea monster underlined Yeshua's universal mission which exploded the narrow confines of Palestinian Judaism in the first centuries of our era.

This co-opting of paradigmatic Hebrew Bible figures and motifs in circulation during the first centuries CE squares nicely with a Near Eastern milieu, since the appropriation of motifs can be seen throughout the ancient Near East. Even the God of Israel is known to have appropriated some of the attributes of other gods as well as their domains as part of the process of emergent monotheism.

What follows reveals some of the sources upon which New Testament writers drew. Chapter 1 discusses the ancient Near Eastern scribal practice of making use of appropriated templates, using a variety of examples, including biblical ones. Chapter 2 is an examination of the creation sea monster motif and its co-opting for use in the proclamation of Yeshua's divinity. Chapter 3 demonstrates that Yeshua's miracles reproduce those attributed to Elijah and Elisha. Chapter 4 provides examples whereby the method of theological argumentation applied to Yeshua offers a deeper understanding of certain New Testament texts.

This brief work is based on insights gleaned from the work of others. The ideas are not new, but they are articulated in a new way to give them a clear slant toward my presumption that wholeheartedly agrees with what New Testament writers sought to convey: that Yeshua was, indeed, God incarnate who brought salvation to all humanity.

Reading Yeshua's miracles against the signs and wonders performed by Elijah and Elisha steers clear of the issue of historicity. The historicity of miracles is beyond the scope of the present study, as much as it is beyond the ability of historical inquiry. The quest for the historical Jesus has kept generations of biblical scholars busy trying to identify what Yeshua actually did, and what his followers said he did. Such a split between events and their interpretation has not proven very fruitful because it goes against the grain of tradition. The Bible, as much as any other sacred book, is a library. Libraries are the result of a long process of accumulation, borrowing, and appropriation of elements from different horizons and periods. The whole is superior to the sum of the individual parts. Tradition is that whole. Miracles are part of it, even if the notion of miracles contradicts modern concepts of reality. In that sense, the miracles attributed to Yeshua convey as much meaning as his sermons, irrespective of what actually occurred.

This book is intended for students of the Bible and believers seeking to nourish their faith with a deeper understanding of who their Lord was as he came to share our human condition in the particular circumstances of first-century Palestine. Though each point made in the following pages can be backed by references to up-to-date publications in the fields of the Hebrew Bible and New Testament, footnotes are provided sparingly, as guidance to further reading on particular points.

I

Appropriation &
Imago Dei Mirrored

A WORLD OF ONGOING APPROPRIATION

Natives of ancient Palestine would have been familiar
with the stories of the Hebrew Bible; members of sectar-
ian groups, priests, and scribes even more so. Despite low
literacy rates, most individuals, irrespective of social class,
would have been conversant with some of the contents of
the growing corpus of sacred texts that would later become
the Hebrew Bible. The stories recorded in the Hebrew Bible
were likely recited and preached, and they would have
resonated with the majority on a variety of levels. It is not
surprising that those stories were drawn upon when what
eventually became the Christian Scriptures were penned.
Those images and figures were used to articulate who
Yeshua was, what he did, and how he came to fulfill the
Hebrew Scriptures. Appropriation, or the use of exemplars,

is commonplace in ancient religious texts because it was an ancient practice that had proven helpful in rooting new ideas into old traditions. This literary technique has been used throughout history, as will be demonstrated below from ancient Near East examples and others extending beyond its milieu to our own day.

As modern examples, phrases such as "he/she hit a home run," or "that was a curve ball" may be heard in regard to something totally unrelated to baseball. Such sport imagery is used in contexts unrelated to sport. With these modern examples of appropriation, imagery pertaining to baseball is used to express ideas in other areas of life. "Hitting a home run" is meaningful in North America, where baseball is popular, but less so elsewhere. In ancient Palestine, a similar idea would have drawn on another repertoire of images. Hence, to express religious notions, Yeshua's teaching often uses agricultural metaphors that contained meaning that was transparent to his audience. Appropriation pertains to ideas and images, but also to space.

Sacred Space

Perhaps most prominently observable to modern eyes are examples where sacred space and artistic motifs are appropriated and reused. Sanctuaries erected by one religious tradition are sometimes taken over and used by another tradition. For example, Greco-Roman temples were later made into churches. In the Middle East, some of these churches were then turned into mosques, as happened to the Hagia Sophia in Istanbul. The function of the building remains, though the religious identity of the worshipers changed. The change sometimes involved minimal alterations to the structure of the building. The replacement of some religious symbols can suffice to assert the claim of the sanctuary by the new power.

Art & Iconography

A salient example of the appropriation of art comes to the fore with the well-known image or motif known as the *manus Dei* or *dextera domini*, the hand of God or right hand of God in English. This motif is frequently used in depictions of Yeshua in paintings as well as statues (Figure 1).

The origins of the motif may go back to the ancient Near East, and became prominent in Judeo-

Figure 1

Christian religious spheres, particularly well attested in artistic representations from Palmyra, Syria. For instance, a eunuch (?) had himself pictured on his funerary relief with his right hand at heart level with two middle fingers bent (Figure 2).

On another funerary plaque (Figure 3), a servant stands behind his mistress and does the same gesture, but with his left hand, probably because his right

Figure 2

hand is hidden behind the *grande dame* in order to show her prominence.

Figure 3

Figure 4

One of the faces of a first-century altar from the Baal Shamin sanctuary, also from Palmyra, shows the goddess Allat with her right hand raised and palm stretched outward (Figure 4). The *dextera domini* motif appears as a later combination of these Palmyrean types in Christian iconography.[1] Yeshua is displayed with a slightly elevated right arm at heart level, with thumb

1. Hachlili, *Ancient Jewish Art*, 145, mentions a Palmyrean altar with four upraised hands with the palms outwards, quoting Tanabe, *Sculptures of Palmyra*, Pl. 152.

and forefinger making a circle while the other fingers appear relaxed and pointed slightly upward. There are variations in the manner the motif is displayed, though the gesture is generally understood to convey blessing by a holy figure, Yeshua, or saints of the Catholic and Orthodox traditions.

The motif appears in non-Abrahamic faith traditions, the Buddha being a most notable example whose portrayal with a similar gesture is ubiquitous (Figure 5). Irrespective of where and when it originated, Jews, Christians, and Buddhists appropriated the *manus Dei* motif for their respective religious figures. Though there is of course no evidence that Yeshua ever made this gesture himself,

Figure 5

artists used it to convey his divine status. Therefore, the *manus Dei* is one example of the appropriation of a motif by different cultures.

Another well-known appropriation in Christian iconography is the Egyptian scene called "Isis lactans." The Egyptian goddess Isis, a very popular figure in late Antiquity, was often represented breast-feeding the young Osiris, destined to become the next Pharaoh. The theme of the Blessed Virgin holding the Christ Child on her lap has enjoyed as much popularity in Christian art as that of Isis as divine mother, both epitomes of motherhood.

Modern Lives of Yeshua

Modern-day reenactments of Yeshua in movies and paintings show cultural borrowings or appropriation, but in a different manner. The borrowing goes from the present to the past, causing anachronisms. It is an example of borrowing that betrays Yeshua and his context in light of the period in which the art or movie was produced. Ironically, his disciples are always painted and portrayed in conformity with the outfits, costumes, imagery of the era of the artists, and not how first-century Palestinians would have actually looked or dressed. For example, Yeshua is often portrayed wearing long hair. Such a hairstyle is unlikely, considering Paul argues in 1 Corinthians 11:14 that it was shameful for men to have long hair. The letter reflects the cultural conventions and contexts of Paul, who ministered soon after Yeshua's death.

The blue-eyed white Anglo-Saxon in Roman garb is a fixture of Jesus movies. It is an unlikely representation of Yeshua's actual earthly looks, but a crucial one for the identification of the audience with the film's hero.

ANCIENT NEAR EASTERN DEITIES

The Israelite God, Yahweh

There is a consensus among Hebrew Bible scholars that the Lord, or Yahweh, appropriated other divine entities and their domains as part of the process leading toward Yahwistic monotheism.[2] As part of the process of emergent monotheism, it was requisite that, to become the sole deity, the head of the pantheon took over the attributes, characters, and prerogatives that were ascribed to the other

2. See Anderson, *Monotheism and Yahweh's Appropriation*.

gods. Appropriation was necessary and its occurrence left a legacy that reverberates today among the three Abrahamic faiths. Judaism, Christianity, and Islam owe much to this process of appropriation, which eventually led to the portrayal of the Lord as the one and only true god.

In ancient Israel and Judah, the god Baal was thought to control the weather, a crucial domain in an agrarian society entirely dependent on irregular Mediterranean rain levels. The Hebrew Bible accuses the ancient Israelites of Baal worship. To make the case that the Lord is the true god, the Hebrew Bible does not shy away from portraying Yahweh in the image of Baal, as the one bringing rain and fertility to the land. Instead of arguing that there are no such things as weather gods, or negating the existence of Baal, the Hebrew scribes presented Yahweh under the traits of Baal, thus appropriating Baal's domain for Yahweh and making Baal redundant.

Traces of this process of appropriation are found in the different names the Hebrew Bible uses for the God of Israel, many of which originally signified different deities, but which were eventually subsumed to become synonyms for the Lord. The sole God swallowed up the others.

The Assyrian God, Assur, and the Babylonian God, Marduk

In the struggle for supremacy, the Israelite God was not alone in appropriating the domains and names of other gods. In Mesopotamia, both Assur, the Assyrian head god, and Marduk, the Babylonian head god, usurped the domain of the chief god, Enlil, by being portrayed in the image of Enlil.[3] Though Marduk had long been known as

3. Na'aman, "Israelite-Judahite Struggle," 9.

a fairly insignificant god within the pantheon under En-lil, his ascendancy corresponded with the political rise of Babylon.[4] With the ascendancy of ancient cities, in this case Assur and Babylon, their respective patron deities were promoted to the highest rank by appropriating the attributes of the chief deity and the domains of the other members of the pantheon.

As Babylon rose to a position of prominence over the other cities of Mesopotamia and ruled over most of the ancient Near East, so too did its head deity, Marduk, rise to a similar position of dominance. The same had happened earlier with the chief god of the Assyrians. In Babylon, appropriation was signified by listing the attributes and symbols associated with different deities and attributing them to Marduk. The best-known example of this development is captured by a Late Babylonian tablet currently housed at the British Museum. It reads:

> Uras (is) Marduk of planting
> Lugalidda (is) Marduk of the abyss
> Ninurta (is) Marduk of the pickax
> Nergal (is) Marduk of battle
> Zababa (is) Marduk of warfare
> Enlil (is) Marduk of lordship and consultations
> Nabu (is) Marduk of accounting
> Sin (is) Marduk who lights up the night
> Samas (is) Marduk of justice
> Adad (is) Marduk of rain
> Tispak (is) Marduk of troops
> Great Anu (is) Marduk of [text broken]
> Suqamuna (is) Marduk of the container

4. Abusch, "Marduk," 543–49.

[text broken (is)] Marduk of everything.[5]

There are other Akkadian texts from the Late Babylonian period that contend that other deities are but aspects of Marduk, an idea also present at the end of the Babylonian creation account, *Enuma Elish*.[6] The list of secondary deities there seems to indicate that these gods only exist through Marduk. There are also texts about the god Ninurta that suggest the same idea, that all other gods are aspects of the god being extolled; though one should be cautious in viewing this phenomenon as a type of monotheism, a term commonly understood today in the sense of negating the existence of all but one deity. It was a convention to extol a god, rather than a statement that that god was the only god.

In fact, ancient texts and artifacts abundantly show that all the gods named in the above list are typically portrayed surrounded by an entourage of other gods. The greater the god, the greater the number of divine courtiers around him. Ascribing the attributes of the courtiers to the sovereign was a way to praise the head of the pantheon. Instead of implying any denial of the importance of the divine court, the numerous courtiers proved the greatness of the head deity. Appropriation of divine attributes and domains was a strategy of worship.

Co-opting of Festivals

Just as space was sacred and usurped, so time was sacred and taken over. Holidays and festivals tend to occur at crucial times of the yearly cycle, such as equinoxes and solstices (approximately March/September 21 and June/

---

5. Lambert, "Historical Development," 193.
6. For other examples, see Smith, *God in Translation*, 170–75.

December 21, respectively). While their dates vary little, the significant events they commemorate differ. For instance, before celebrating the birth and death of Christ, Christmas celebrated the return of light and Easter the end of winter, all associated with different deities across the world. The main festivals in the Hebrew Bible are reconfigured agriculture festivals related to the Exodus.[7] Pesah (Passover), Massot (Unleavened bread), and Sukkot (Tabernacles) thus celebrate the release from captivity in Egypt instead of different stages of the harvest, vital events in any agricultural society.

The appropriation of agricultural festivals continued as Christianity co-opted the Jewish festival of Pentecost, which celebrates the gift of the Torah to Moses at Sinai, and turned it into the joyous time when the Holy Spirit descended upon the apostles of Yeshua (Acts 2:1–13). Such appropriations belong to religious patterns that transcend temporal and geographic borders.

Genesis

Further examples of appropriation, this time literary appropriation much like what will be discussed in what follows, can be observed in the creation accounts of the book of Genesis. It has long been known that the first part of Genesis, the so-called Primordial History (Genesis 1–11), is heavily dependent on Mesopotamian motifs. Though direct borrowing cannot be proven, it is overwhelmingly clear that the biblical tower of Babel reflects on the Ziggurats of Mesopotamia.

The biblical flood itself follows Mesopotamian models. While in early creation myths the flood revolved around a

7. Edelman, "Exodus and Pesach/Massot," 169.

river only, it was expanded in later literature to encompass the entire known world, a version of the flood taken over in Genesis, but ascribed to the God of Israel. Hence, Genesis appropriated the attributes of the creator god for the God of Israel.

Ignoring the roles played by Marduk for the Babylonians or by Ahura Mazda for the Persians was not an option if Yahweh was to be elevated above these deities and made the ruler of heaven and earth. It was necessary to use the same motifs in a polemical fashion to show that it is Yahweh who is the creator of the heavens and earth. Literary appropriation of the creator motif that was prevalent when the first part of Genesis was produced was a necessary step before the existence of the other creator gods could be denied entirely. Before making them redundant, these gods had to be figuratively emptied of their substance.

Adam in the Image of Adapa

In light of this appropriation process, it is hardly surprising that the Old Testament figure of Adam is based on an older ancient Near Eastern figure named Adapa. The extant texts mentioning Adapa are by far much older than the book of Genesis. The Sumerian *Adapa*, or its literary avatars, served as the archetype for the Adam of the Hebrews and for the Oannes of the Greeks[8]. The Sumerians understood Adapa to be the first of the antediluvian semi-divine sages. These sages were said to have brought civilization and art to Sumer. Just as Adapa is the first semi-divine being in Sumerian texts, so Adam is the first human in Genesis.

There is, however, an obvious difference in that Adam was not thought to be semi-divine. To underline the

8. Hallo and Simpson, *Ancient Near East*, 28–29.

difference, and thus reserve all divinity for Yahweh, the biblical scribes chose a name for their first human based on the Hebrew word *adamah*, "soil, earth, dirt." Hence, appropriation entailed more than simple mimicking. It was a creative process in its own right.

Yeshua as the New Moses

Before showing that Yeshua is conspicuously patterned after Elijah (see chapter 3), another salient example of appropriation comes by way of the portrayal of Yeshua as the new Moses in the Gospels.[9] As Moses delivered his people from slavery in Egypt, so Yeshua saves and delivers his people from all forms of oppression. Moses and the Exodus generation remain forty years in the wilderness; so must Yeshua spend forty days in the desert. More than once, the Israelites are tempted to give up and return to Egypt, so Yeshua is tempted by Satan in the desert (Luke 4:1–2). This depiction of Yeshua patterned after Moses is a typical example of mirrored *Imago Dei*.

Imago Dei Mirrored

Imago Dei is Latin for "Image of God," the translation of the creation of humankind in God's image in Genesis (Gen 1:26–28; 5:1–3; 9:6). Much theological reflection sought to define what in humanity reflects the divine or what precisely it is in us that derives from the image of God. Is it our soul, our capacity for love? Regardless of the answer, that we are somehow created in God's image is confessional for virtually all Christian denominations. What

9. Allison, *New Moses*; Moessner, "Luke 9:1–50," 565–606.

"image" means is no simple matter. The Hebrew term is more akin to "shadow." As the shadow the sun projects on the ground when its rays hit our body, being the shadow of God on earth evokes the notion of an outline that requires divine light, an outline we are called to fill in with colors and content.

When dealing with Yeshua, the *imago Dei* involved a kind of game of mirrors. The term "mirrored" is used here because in some instances the writers of the New Testament portrayed Yeshua not in the image of God, but rather in the image of humans. Since humans were created in the image of God, presenting Yeshua in the image of human figures such as Elijah and Moses expressed that he was God. As Yeshua was painted in the image of humans, the expression "*imago Dei* mirrored" designates the process by which Yeshua was truly *Immanuel*, literally "God with us." A similar mirroring process is at work with the title "Son of Man." As mirror of *imago Dei*, the divinity of Yeshua is in some instances patterned after great human figures of the past. From a Christian perspective, we confess that Yeshua was both human and divine.

To conclude this chapter, the process of appropriation entails different avenues and types. It was and remains a widespread technique to borrow from different eras and cultures in order to make a statement for one's own time and place. This is done the world over. In the examples of space and time reviewed above, the sacred element remains. It is taken over and reconfigured.

Essentially, Yeshua is modeled after great figures of the Old Testament, in particular Elijah and Elisha, to express his humanity. But as the stories of Elijah and Elisha unfold away from the Sea of Galilee, the evangelists selected another motif to express Yeshua's divinity.

2

Monsters, Chaos, and Yeshua

THE MOTIF OF A deity fighting a sea monster was ubiquitous in the ancient Near East. Thousands of seals and drawings depicting a god battling with the sea or a sea monster have been excavated. Besides these artifacts, tablets recording such mythical battles have been found, the most notable example being the Babylonia Creation account, or Enuma Elish as it is designated according to its initial words, literally "When on high."

The sea, with its dangerous waters, was a metaphor for chaos in Assyrian, Babylonian, and Canaanite literature. With their primitive boats, fishermen and sailors feared the violent gales of the Mediterranean as much as the storms on the Sea of Galilee and the annual flooding of the Euphrates and Tigris Rivers. These waters were perceived as indomitable forces.

GOD'S BATTLE WITH THE SEA MONSTER IN THE HEBREW BIBLE

Monsters were thought to inhabit the sea. Texts from the city of Ugarit (today Ras Shamra in Northern Syria) describe at great length Baal's fight with the sea monster Yam. With weapons prepared by another god, Baal (Baʻlu in Ugaritic) eventually manages to vanquish his foe Yammu/Naharu:

> So the mace whirls in Baʻlu's
> hand, like a hawk
> in his fingers,
>
> Strikes Prince Yammu
> on the head,
>
> Ruler Naharu Baal
> on the forehead.
>
> Yammu goes groggy,
> falls to the ground;
>
> His joints go slack,
> his body slumps.
>
> Baʻlu grabs Yammu and sets
> about dismembering him,
> sets about finishing Ruler
> Naharu off.[1]

Only a young and impetuous god such as Baal, whose nickname is "the Bull," could conquer the forces of chaos

Figure 6

represented by the sea. A stele found at Ugarit displays Baal standing on his pedestal in the shape of a bull, trampling the billowing sea (Figure 6).

1. Pardee "Baʻlu Myth," 249.

15

Baal's hard-won victory over chaos was the prerequisite for the creation of our world. As the Babylonians named their supreme god Marduk rather than Baal, the Babylonian creation account, Enuma Elish (already mentioned in chapter 1), describes Marduk's battle against Tiamat, the Babylonian name for the sea monster and symbol of the primeval chaos. The biblical scribes were somehow aware of Tiamat's name and imagery since Genesis twice designates the precreational state of the world with unusual words that recall Tiamat's name: "The earth was a formless void (Hebrew *tohu wa bohu*) and darkness covered the face of the deep (Hebrew *tehom*), while a wind from God swept over the face of the waters" (Gen 1:2). *Tehom* is none other than the masculine form of the feminine name *Tiamat*.

The biblical *tohu wa bohu* and *tehom* are not divine entities any more. They need not be struck and dismembered. The biblical Creator does not even need to fight them. Yet, his wind (or Spirit) has to sweep over (literally "to hover over") the waters and dominate them before his creative words can be pronounced. Then, the chaos is organized into orderly time cycles (days and weeks) and inhabitable space (water, dry land, and skies). With the idea that the world was created by ordering a preexisting chaos, Genesis 1 remains closer to the ancient Near Eastern creation myths than the later philosophical notion of *creation ex nihilo* ("creation out of nothing") would suggest.

The Hebrew Bible also transmits allusions to other figures known from Ugaritic creation myths. These include the goddess Anat, who helped Baal defeat the sea monster, who also goes by the names of Motu ("Death"), Rahab ("Rage, Surge"), and Lotan. Ugaritic "Lotan" becomes "Leviathan" in Hebrew:

> You divided the sea by your might; you broke the heads of the dragons in the waters. You crushed the heads of Leviathan; you gave him as food for the creatures of the wilderness. You cut openings for springs and torrents; you dried up ever-flowing streams. (Ps 74:13–15)

> On that day Yahweh with his cruel and great and strong sword will punish Leviathan the fleeing serpent, Leviathan the twisting serpent, and he will kill the dragon that is in the sea. (Isa 27:1)

Rahab is mentioned in poetical texts that recall the sea monster motif:

> Awake, awake, put on strength, O arm of Yahweh! Awake, as in days of old, the generations of long ago! Was it not you who cut Rahab in pieces, who pierced the dragon? Was it not you who dried up the sea, the waters of the great deep; who made the depths of the sea a way for the redeemed to cross over? (Isa 51:9–10)

> You crushed Rahab like a carcass. (Ps 89:7)

> By his power he stilled the Sea; by his understanding he struck down Rahab. By his wind the heavens were made fair; his hand pierced the fleeing serpent. (Job 26:12–13)

Other biblical allusions to the battle with the sea monster include Psalm 104:25–27, and Job 40:15–41.

There is little doubt that the sea monster motif has been appropriated in the Hebrew Bible in a polemical way to make the point that it was Yahweh who defeated primeval chaos, not Baal, Marduk, or any other god. The motif was resonant enough to reappear at the end of the Christian Bible, as a great serpent who pours water like a flood (Rev 12:15) until he is seized and bound (Rev 20:2).

YESHUA AND THE BATTLE WITH THE SEA MONSTER IN THE NEW TESTAMENT

One need not wait until the book of Revelation for the motif of the divine battle with the sea dragon to recur. The motif serves to extol Yeshua in the first Gospel, when Yeshua stills a storm by walking on the Sea of Galilee (Matt 14:22–33).

Yeshua's walk on water is more than a mere feat to impress the disciples. Yeshua rides the mighty waves that battered the disciples' boat all night and frightened Peter when he tried to imitate his master. Like the depiction of Baal on the Ugarit Stele (Figure 6), Yeshua tramples the chaotic waters that symbolize the primeval sea monster. Hence, there is more in this passage than a miracle of walking atop water. Trampling mighty waves, Yeshua is depicted as the true god, the one who conquers the waters of chaos. Much meaning is lost if, unaware of the mythological motifs of the ancient Near East, the reader remains focused on the miracle of walking on water. The disciples were terrified when they first saw Yeshua coming toward them because, behind the waves, it was the god who stirred the lake against them that they feared. And in this they were correct! At last, they confessed "Truly you are the Son of God."

Because only gods were understood to have the ability to vanquish the sea, the deeper meaning of the miracle is that Yeshua is the true God who not only conquers the waters that symbolize chaos and dark forces, but he also stands over and above the chaos and tramples the monster that stirs the sea. Whereas it took Baal and Marduk painstaking encounters with the dragons, Yeshua stills the sea by the simple act of trampling its billows, to demonstrate that dark powers do not faze him. Calming the sea is a claim of divinity for Yeshua (Matt 8:26; Mark 4:39; Luke 8:24). Trampling enemies is also a common motif in Assyrian and Egyptian art where the king places a foot on the defeated enemy, or four feet when Pharaoh is depicted as a sphinx (Figure 7).

Figure 7

3

Yeshua as the New Elijah

As noted in Chapter 1, Yeshua was portrayed as the new Moses in the Gospels of Matthew and Luke. The Gospels also portray him as the new Elijah. In fact, the Gospel of Mark displays Yeshua performing many of the miracles ascribed to Elijah and Elisha. Elijah himself is depicted as another Moses, a point particularly clear in 1 Kings 19 where Elijah encounters God on Mount Horeb. As Elijah's successor, Elisha imitates some of his master's miracles.[1] Hence, in the footsteps of Raymond Brown, Thomas Brodie identified the Elijah-Elisha narrative as one of the literary precedents of the Gospels.[2]

THE NAMES

The names of Elijah and Elisha are significant. Like the name Michael, which means "Who is like God," Elijah is

---

1. See Ghantous, *Elisha-Hazael Paradigm*, 125.
2. Brodie, *Crucial Bridge*; Brown, "Jesus and Elisha," 86–104.

composed of two divine elements, El "God" and "Yah," a diminutive for Yahweh, the God of Israel. "Elijah" thus means "My God is Yahweh" or "Yahweh is (the only) God," appropriate designations for a prophet who wages war against the prophets of Baal in (1 Kings 18) to prove that Yahweh rather than Baal is the true Storm God who sends rain and protects Israel from drought-induced famines.

Elisha means "El/God saves." It is hardly a coincidence that "Yeshua" means "Yah(weh) saves," though the biblical Joshua and Josiah bear names with similar meanings based on the same verb. Elisha, Joshua, and Josiah brought salvation in one way or another, but it is to Elisha (and Elijah) that the Gospels turned most to portray Yeshua's ministry.

THE MIRACLES

The fact that, for Christians, the salvation enacted by Yeshua's sacrifice suffers no comparison with any other religious figure, biblical or other, should not make modern readers blind to the way the Gospel writers used their Scriptures to portray Yeshua. For Jews and Christians of the first centuries of our era, Holy Scripture comprised more or less what came to be designated by Christians as the Old Testament. After the five books of the Torah (or the Law in Christian Bibles), came the Prophets introduced by works dedicated to Israel's past after the Exodus, i.e., Joshua, Judges, Samuel, and Kings, books designated as "historical" in Christian Bibles. Modern Bible editions split the books of Samuel and Kings in two (1 and 2 Samuel; 1 and 2 Kings) though the old Greek translations of these books considered them as one (1 to 4 Kingdoms). The Elijah-Elisha narrative extends from Elijah's announcement of a severe drought in 1 Kings 17 to the death of Elisha in 2 Kings 13.

The following chart (Table 1) lists all the miracles (signs and wonders taken in a broad sense) performed by Elijah and Elisha with references to those performed by Yeshua in the Gospels and in some cases in the Book of Acts.[3]

1 Kgs		Mark	Matt	Luke
13:4–7	Paralyzed hand healed	3:1–6	12:9–14	6:6–11
17:6	Fed by ravens/being with wild beasts	1:13		
17:8–9	Multiplying oil and flour/fish and bread	6:41 + John 6:11	14:16	9:16
17:17–18	Raising a son from the dead			7:11
19:6	Fed by an angel/fasting in the desert	1:13	4:1	4:2
2 Kgs				
1:10–12	Fire from heaven			9:54
2:13	Magical mantle	5:28; 6:56	9:21	8:44
2:14	Waters cut/walked over	6:45 + John 6:18	14:22–33	
2:20	Healing salt	9:50?	5:13?	14:34?
2:23–24	Children torn/invited	10:13	19:13–15	18:15–17
4:1–7	Multiplying oil/bread and fish	8:6	15:36	
4:18–37	Raising a son/daughter from the dead	5:41	9:25	8:50
4:38	Healing pottage with flour			
4:41–44	Multiplication of bread	8:6	15:36	
5:1–19	Naaman's leprosy healed	1:40	8:1–4	5:12–16
5:9–27	Gehazi's leprosy/Ananias struck dead			Acts 5
6:17–20	Eyes opened	8:25	9:30; 23:30	Act 9:18

Table 1: Synopsis of miracles
performed by Elijah, Elisha, and Yeshua

3. Guillaume, "Miracles Miraculously Repeated," 21. Brodie, *Birthing of the New Testament*, 39–42.

Not all miraculous deeds recorded in the Elijah-Elisha narrative are reproduced in the Gospels. Reading Yeshua's miracles against the background of the Elijah-Elisha narrative reveals what the evangelists considered inappropriate. The military feats that involve Elisha in the wars between Aram and Israel have no obvious Gospel parallels. Those are the red waters (2 Kgs 3:16), spying on the King of Aram (2 Kgs 6:8), and the blinding of Aramean soldiers (2 Kgs 6:18). The sanitizing of a poisonous spring and of a pottage (2 Kgs 2:19; 4:41), as well as the floating ax head (2 Kgs 6:6), are equally without direct echoes in the Gospels, though the various references to the "salt of the earth" may be indirect references. By contrast, the healing of King Jeroboam's hand in 1 Kings 13:6 is echoed in the Synoptic Gospels (Matthew, Mark, Luke), though it is performed by an anonymous man of God from Judah rather than by Elijah or Elisha. Therefore, to the Gospel writers, the books of Kings formed a unit (or narrative cycle) within which the miracle of 1 Kings 13 was as important as those performed by Elijah or Elisha. Though Elisha's military feats are avoided, the sequel of the blinding of the Aramean soldiers found its way as the healing of a blind man (Mark 8:25, with parallels in Matthew, Mark, and Acts).

Apart from these, most of the miracles performed by Yeshua in the Gospels reflect episodes of the Elijah-Elisha Cycle. The Gospel of Mark follows this collection of miracles so closely that it clearly served as its template. Twelve of Mark's eighteen or so miracles have parallels in Elijah-Elisha. The only miracles in Mark without clear parallels in Kings are healings (Mark 2:11; 4:32–34; 6:56; 7:34), the stilling of the storm (Mark 4:39), and the exorcism of a demoniac (Mark 5:13).

The other Gospels reshuffled the miracles of Elijah and Elisha according to their own narrative logic. Overall, each Gospel includes a dozen of the twenty or so miracles found in Kings. Exorcisms compensate for missing miracles.

The evangelists did not follow the Elijah-Elisha template in a slavish manner. For instance, the chilling revenge brought about by two she-bears on forty boys who taunted Elisha for his baldness is turned upside-down with Yeshua's call to let young children come to him (2 Kgs 2:24; Matt 19:14; Mark 10:14; Luke 18:16).

The Elijah-Elisha template explains the duplication of certain miracles. Elijah multiplies flour and oil at Zarephath (1 Kgs 17:16). Elisha multiplies the oil of the widow of a son of the prophets (2 Kgs 4:6) and barley loaves for a hundred men (2 Kgs 4:44). Matthew and Mark thus ascribe two multiplications of bread and fish to Yeshua, but for greater numbers (5,000 and 4,000 men). Luke considered that one multiplication was sufficient. Yet, Luke compensated it with a second raising from the dead, the young man in Nain (Luke 7:15). This miracle has no parallel in the other Gospels, but it reproduces the raising of a child by both Elijah and Elisha (1 Kgs 17:22; 2 Kgs 4:35). Luke created more parallels of his own. For instance, between the fire from heaven, which burns the soldiers who try to arrest Elijah (2 Kgs 1:10–12), and the fire James and John want to rain on a Samaritan village (Luke 9:55). Table 2 indicates other Lukan parallels.

While the Elijah-Elisha template enabled the evangelists to state that Yeshua was both the new Elijah and the new Elisha, some miracles were improved to reveal that Yeshua is greater than both. Besides the number of people fed thanks to the multiplication of bread and fish discussed above, Yeshua fasted throughout his forty days in the desert, contrary to Elijah, who was fed by ravens at the Wadi Cherith and by an angel on his way to Horeb.

How many miracles Yeshua actually performed is not the point. All we will ever know is that the New Testament is ambiguous regarding miracles. Given the plethora of miracle-workers at the time, signs and wonders did not set Yeshua's ministry apart from other self-appointed messiahs (Matt 24:24; Mark 13:22). John 3:2 implies that the miracles performed by Yeshua were greater than those of his contemporaries, though two chapters later, John has Yeshua resisting the populace's thirst for healing (John 4:48). The apostle Paul was also aware that miracles in themselves could not signify the uniqueness of Yeshua's mission (1 Cor 1:22). The evangelists, therefore, turned to Elijah and Elisha to legitimize their portrayal of Yeshua as a miracle worker. In this way, they remained within the bounds established by their template.

OTHER EPISODES

While the Gospel writers used the miracles of the Elijah-Elisha cycle with moderation, they also found other themes and details that are not miracles as such. The next chart (Table 2) lists episodes and expressions in the Elijah-Elisha cycle, which have parallels in the New Testament, mostly in the Gospels.

1 Kgs		Mark	Matt	Luke
11:40	Fleeing to Egypt		2:13–15	
13:10	Return by a different way		2:12	
13:30	Laying a corpse in one's own grave		27:60	
17:18	"What have you to do with me/us?"	5:7 + John 2:4	8:29	8:28
19:8–18	Divine encounter	9:2–9 + 2 Pet 1:17	17:1–9	9:28–36
19:19–21	Calling disciple(s)	1:20	4:18–22; 8:22	4:14; 9:60–62; 14:26
2 Kgs				
1:8	Leather belt	1:6	3:6	
1:9–10	Soldiers sent to arrest	14:43 + John 18:3	26:47–56	22:47–53
2:4–5	"I will not leave you"		8:19	9:57
2:11	Ascension	16:19		24:51
4:8–10	Entourage of rich women			8:3
4:29	Staff/no staff	6:8	10:10	9:3
6:19	"Follow me!"	1:17; 2:13	4:19–21; 9:9	5:11, 27
9:13	Carpet of cloaks for the new king	11:8	21:8	19:36

**Table 2: Motifs and phrases from the
Elijah-Elisha cycle in the New Testament**

Less contrived than they were with the delicate matter of miracles, the evangelists deployed much creativity in the elaboration of other motifs they found in the Elijah-Elisha template. In fact, the Elijah-Elisha template led the evangelists to go beyond the confines of the chapters of the books of Kings that narrate the deeds of Elijah and Elisha. The previous section has shown that the Gospels ascribe to Yeshua the healing of a hand that echoes the healing of King Jeroboam's hand performed by an anonymous prophet.

In the same way, Matthew combined two separate motifs from King Jeroboam's life to fill in the story of Yeshua's infancy that Mark ignores. The first of these motifs is the magi's return home by conscientiously avoiding Jerusalem and Herod.

Returning Another Way

That the magi should avoid Jerusalem on their way back home (Matt 2:12) makes sense as Herod was trying to murder the newborn king. Yet, that detail is somewhat redundant since the next verse explains that upon the wise men's departure Joseph also received a warning and was instructed to flee to Egypt to foil Herod's plan (Matt 2:13). Matthew could easily have had the newborn Yeshua saved from the Bethlehem slaughter thanks to the warning sent to Joseph only. The other warning sent to the wise men thus reinforces the first link with 1 Kings 13, the episode of the man of God from Judah who came to Bethel to oppose King Jeroboam. Hence, to the parallels with the healing of the paralyzed hand (1 Kgs 13:6; Matt 12:13; Mark 3:6; Luke 6:10), Matthew adds the magi's return by another way as well as a third parallel. After healing Jeroboam's hand, the man of God from Judah is tricked by an old prophet of Bethel, and is punished by a lion that kills him. The trickster then places the man of God in his own grave (1 Kgs 13:30). Joseph of Arimathea who places Yeshua's body in his own new grave is a clear echo of the prophet of Bethel (1 Kgs 13:30; Matt 27:60).

Instead of this link with the old prophet of Bethel, a more direct link could have been made with Elisha's own grave. A man whose body happened to be hurriedly thrown into Elisha's tomb was instantly resurrected when his body touched Elisha's bones (2 Kgs 13:21). Matthew considered this pointer to Yeshua's resurrection too obvious. He preferred a roundabout approach. The tomb of the old prophet of Bethel is remembered by King Josiah, who spared it when he emptied the other tombs to desecrate the altar of Bethel by burning human bones on it (2 Kgs 23:17). The detour via Bethel adds an element of royalty to Yeshua's burial, since Joseph of Arimathea is only deemed a rich man (Matt 27:57) or a respected member of the council (Mark 15:43). This intricate interweaving of motifs from different Old Testament episodes to produce multilayered scenes is discussed further in chapter 4.

Fleeing to Egypt

After the magi's discovery of the child, Matthew continues with the magi's avoidance of Jerusalem to avoid informing Herod about the location of the newborn king. When Herod realizes he had been tricked, he orders a general slaughter of the children of Bethlehem in the hope that Mary's child will be among the victims (Matt 2:19). Forewarned by an angel, however, Joseph has already left for Egypt with Mary and her child. This escape echoes Jeroboam who fled to King Shishak of Egypt when Solomon sought to kill him (1 Kgs 11:40; 12:2). Jeroboam and the holy family remained in Egypt until they were informed of the death of their enemy (1 Kgs 12:2; Matt 2:13, 19–21).

"What Is There Between Us?"

Though the NRSV has the widow of Zarephath ask "What have you *against* me, O man of God?" (1 Kgs 17:18), the term "against" is an interpretation based on the idea that the woman seems to rebuke Elijah because her son is about to die. The Greek translation of this verse renders the Hebrew phrase "what for me and for you" exactly (Τί ἐμοὶ καὶ σοί). Given the importance of the Greek translation of the Old Testament for the New Testament writers, it is hardly surprising that the widow's question to Elijah is found as such in the Gospels but set in entirely different contexts. Mirroring the idea that Elijah's encounter with the widow occurred beyond the narrow confines of Palestine proper, on the Southern Lebanese coast at Zarephath, Mark 5:7 and Luke 8:28 put the widow's question in the mouth of a man possessed by an unclean spirit Yeshua met on the other side of the Sea of Galilee, in the land of the Gerasenes.

John 2:4 has Yeshua's mother utter the widow's question at Cana in Galilee when she urges her son to do something about the shortage of wine. John, Mark, and Luke reproduce the widow's question word for word, while Matthew 8:29 (see also Mark 1:24) merely changes the pronoun "me" to "us" since he has two demoniacs instead of one.

In the Synoptic Gospels, the man is said to dwell in tombs. This is a redundant detail, unless the reader picks up in the possessed man's question another allusion to the widow of Zarephath and to her dying son. In this framework, what the man is asking when he comes out of the tombs to meet Yeshua on the lakeside is crucial. What has this man to do with Yeshua? What have they got in common? The answer is that when his own hour will come, Yeshua will come out of the tomb too. The association, however, is only possible because of the prior identification of Yeshua with the son of the widow of Zarephath, which supplies the necessary link with the notion of resurrection.

The Gospel of John picks up the reference to Elijah and applies it to Mary to the same effect. Placing Mary in the place of the widow of Zarephath, John hints at Mary's widowhood. More importantly, Yeshua holds the place of the widow's dying son whom Elijah is going to bring back to life. Each Gospel uses the allusion to Elijah as a hint to Yeshua's ultimate victory over death.

One may doubt the existence of such literary mirror games in the Gospels and argue that the question "What is there between you and me" is too common to be a clear allusion to Elijah. The question is indeed found elsewhere, in the mouth of Jephthah, David, and Pharaoh Neco (Judg 11:12; 2 Sam 16:10, 19:23; 2 Chr 35:21). Yet, only the allusion to the widow of Zarephath makes sense with regard to Yeshua.

Transfiguration

One explicit reference to Elijah is found in the episode of Yeshua's transfiguration on a (high) mountain (Matt 17:1–9; Mark 9:2–9; Luke 9:28–36). More than the others, Matthew's version elaborates on Yeshua's relation to Elijah. In answer of the disciples' question about the scribes' claim that Elijah must come first, Yeshua insists that Elijah has already arrived. With the concluding statement that the disciples understood that Elijah was John the Baptist (Matt 17:13), Matthew hints that in fact Yeshua is Elijah rather than the new Moses.[4] To underline the importance of the Elijah-Elisha cycle as his template, Mark names Elijah before Moses (Mark 9:4). The lawgiver is made secondary to

4. Puig i Tàrrech, "Glory on the Mountain," 151–72.

the miracle worker. Prophecy prevails over law. Yeshua's transfiguration does draw on Moses' encounter with the Lord at Mount Sinai: Moses' radiant face, the trio of followers (Aaron, Nadab, and Abihu in Exodus 24:9; Peter, James, and John in the Gospels), and the cloud-covered mountain (Exod 24:15). Once the parallel with Sinai is established, the figure of Moses is eclipsed by the figure of Elijah who had a divine encounter at Mount Horeb (1 Kgs 19:8). Mark 9:3 insists that only Yeshua's clothing became dazzling white and that the transfiguration lasted but a short time (Mark 9:8). The other Synoptic Gospels use a different strategy. Matthew 17:2 states that Yeshua's face shone like the sun, Luke 9:29 only that his face changed. Both imply that, contrary to Moses, Yeshua never had to veil his face.

The lack of veil is a hint that divine revelation in Christianity is of a higher level than in Judaism. In the transfiguration scene, Peter's proposal to build three dwellings remains rooted in the Old Testament as it alludes to the Feast of Tabernacles (Lev 23:34). Peter's proposal is interrupted by the cloud and his offer is ignored. Mark 9:6 even insists that Peter did not know what he was talking about. Ignoring the Elijah model and focusing solely on Moses leads readers to overinterpret some details and miss the core.

Having established that the figure of Moses is secondary to Elijah's, the presence of Moses *and* Elijah besides Yeshua undercuts any belief that Yeshua may be Moses or Elijah incarnate. Yeshua is more than these two great figures of the Old Testament.

Calling Disciples: "Follow Me"

The four Gospels have Yeshua calling disciples, scenes that very closely follow Elijah's calling of Elisha from behind his plowing team (1 Kgs 19:19–21). Mark retains the urgency of the call and insists that the first disciples immediately drop their nets to follow Yeshua, adding that James and John leave their father behind in the boat (Mark 1:20). Matthew follows Mark very closely, while Luke elaborates the scene with a speech in which Yeshua recalls Elijah's and Elisha's dealings with the widow of Zarephath and Naaman the Syrian to justify his mission to the non-Jews (Luke 4:25–27).

Whereas Elisha's calling required no words—it was enough for Elijah to throw his mantle over Elisha—the evangelists repeatedly reproduce the formula "Follow me" from 2 Kings 6:19 whenever Yeshua is calling disciples. Though the Greek verb is not the same, the idea is similar. Instead of a mere play on words, it creates an elaborate interplay with two other scenes in which Elijah asks Elisha *not* to follow him, though he is about to be taken away (2 Kgs 2:2–4). Elisha disobeys and is thus able to pick up Elijah's mantle and continue his work, whereas the disciples follow Yeshua by obeying the call "Follow me," which Elisha had addressed to the Aramean soldiers who had come to arrest him. Having blinded them, Elisha then leads the soldiers right into Samaria, the capital of their Israelite enemy, on the pretext of leading them to the man they were looking for. Instead of slaughtering the Syrian soldiers, Elisha orders the King of Israel to prepare a great feast for them before setting them free. This adds yet another layer of meaning to the call of Yeshua's disciples. They are later sent to release many from demons, at first only to the lost sheep of Israel (Matt 10:8), but eventually to the entire world. The hometown of the

Aramean soldiers, Damascus, holds a special position as the place where the apostle Paul becomes, against his will, the apostle to the gentiles (Acts 9).

"Let the Dead Bury Their Own Dead"

Less obvious, but no less revealing, is the hint to Elisha's request to kiss his father and mother before following Elijah (1 Kgs 19:20). Elijah's reply "Go back; for what have I done to you?" is given a far more radical twist in Matthew 8:22 and Luke 9:60: "Let the dead bury their own dead." That these words occur in the context of the call of disciples leaves no doubt that they recall Elisha's request. Yet, contrary to Elijah's reply, Yeshua's makes little practical sense. As the dead cannot bury the dead, this saying has even been deemed absurd.[5] A few church fathers grappled with this radical saying, applying it to the life of the Christian community.[6] Yet, the main function of this saying is to mark out the radical nature of Christian discipleship as exceeding the prophetic call in the Hebrew Scriptures. The Gospels actually provide several practical applications of this radical saying. Remaining close to Elisha's mention of his father and mother, Matthew 10:37 has Yeshua state that whoever loves father, mother, son, or daughter more than him is not worthy of him. Luke 14:26 requires *hating* father and mother, wife and children, brothers and sisters, a direct reference to Levi's blessing, who had no regard for his parents, his kin, and his children (Deut 33:9). This verse in Deuteronomy recalls the slaughter of the golden calf worshipers, when Moses ordered the sons of Levi to kill the culprits, even if they were close acquaintances such

5. Konradt, *Das Evangelium Nach Matthaus,* 141.

6. Nicklas, "Let the Dead Bury," 75–90.

as brothers, friends, or neighbors (Exod 32:27). Therefore, the command to hate or to love less must be read in light of apostasy. It only applies when parents, siblings, children, or friends would urge one to reject Christ. This context equally applies to the episode of the visit of Mary to her son.

Yeshua gives a similar harsh answer to those who inform him that his mother is waiting to speak to him—"Who is my mother?"—before pointing to his disciples as standing for his mother because they accomplish his father's will (Matt 12:46; Mark 3:32–33; Luke 8:19–21). Reading these words in light of Elijah's underlines the urgency of the Christian ethos. Reading the same words in light of the golden calf episode adds a crucial corrective. Yeshua does not advocate misanthropy. The target is apostasy and the social pressure family and peers can exert on Yeshua's disciples.

Leather Belts and Hairy Men

The messengers sent by King Ahaziah to consult the god of Ekron describe Elijah as "a hairy man with a leather belt around his waist" (2 Kgs 1:8). Matthew 3:6 and Mark 1:6 describe John the Baptist as clothed with camel's hair, with a leather belt around his waist, eating locusts and wild honey. Mark and Matthew reproduce the Greek words for the "leather belt around his waist" they found in the Septuagint of 2 Kings 1, thus establishing a link between Elijah and John the Baptist. That link, however, is a weak one. Whereas Elijah is a "hairy man," John wears a tunic of camel hair, which relates him to the prophets of Zechariah 13:4, who put on hairy mantles in order to deceive. The evocation of deceiving prophets is a warning. The locusts and wild honey John ate are not associated with Elijah. The baptist shares only one external similarity with Elijah. John is not the new Elijah, only his forerunner.

Arresting Troops

Having identified the hairy man as Elijah, the king sends fifty men to arrest him (2 Kgs 1:9–10). Fire from heaven consumes these soldiers, as well as a second cohort sent to replace them. It is only when the third officer begs Elijah to spare him and his men that Elijah goes to face the king. The Elijah paradigm reveals that in this case the Gospels established a marked difference with Elijah's fiery portrayal. In the Gospels, Judas leads a crowd armed with swords and clubs to arrest Yeshua (Matt 26:43; Mark 14:43; Luke 22:52). John 18:3 has soldiers with lanterns, torches, and weapons, reinforcing the link with the fire imagery in 2 Kings 1. In Matthew 26:51 and Mark 14:43, one of those who stood near draws a sword and cuts the ear of the slave of the high priest. Luke 22:51 adds that Yeshua healed the injured slave. This healing is not found in the other Gospels. Instead, Yeshua orders the culprit to put back his sword for "all who take the sword will perish by the sword" (Matt 26:52). Mark 14:51 has a young man who deserted Yeshua "barely" escape arrest and fleeing naked as his linen cloth was ripped off his back in the ensuing fray. John 18:10 specifies the name of the injured slave, Malchus, a Latin version of the Hebrew and Aramaic word for "King," a hint to the Israelite king who tried to have Elijah arrested.

Each evangelist dealt with the scene of the attempted arrest of Elijah in his own way, but they had Elijah's arrest as the backdrop for Yeshua's arrest. They all resisted attributing to Yeshua Elijah's fire-and-brimstone approach to resistance. Luke is the most intent on the rejection of violence. He added to the healing of the injured slave a scene in which Yeshua rebukes the sons of the thunder (see Mark 3:17) who were eager to command fire from heaven to punish some unwelcoming Samaritans (Luke 9:54). Mark's young man fleeing without his cloak (Mark 14:52) could be an allusion to Elisha's call when Elijah threw his own coat on Elisha (1 Kgs 19:19). The loss of the young man's cloak would thus signify that the violent aspect of Elijah's ministry is not inherited by any follower. Matthew's proverb is based on the proverb of Genesis 9:6, which refers to capital punishment. "He who takes the sword will perish by the sword" (see Revelation 13:10) is an explicit rejection of armed resistance.

Never Shall I Abandon You

On his last trip to Bethel and Jericho, Elijah twice orders Elisha to stay and not to follow him. Elisha protests with a solemn oath twice: "As the LORD lives, and as you yourself live, I will not leave you" (2 Kgs 2:2–4). The Greek verb (καταλείπω), like the Hebrew original (עָזַב), is even stronger: I shall not abandon you! Elisha thus follows Elijah, witnesses his rapture, and inherits Elijah's mantle. While Yeshua is usually calling disciples to follow him, Matthew 8:19 and Luke 9:57 pick up the odd motif of the master who orders his disciple *not* to follow him:

> As they were going along the road, someone said to him, "I will follow you wherever you go." Yeshua replied, "Foxes have holes, and birds of the air have nests; but the Son of Man has nowhere to lay his head."

In both Matthew and Luke, these verses are followed by one (Matt 8:21–22) or two (Luke 9:59–62) opposite cases in which Yeshua calls disciples to follow him. Both ask for a delay, the first to go and bury his father, receiving a sharp answer: "let the dead bury their own dead." The second asks to bid farewell to his relatives and receives an equally harsh answer: "No one who puts a hand to the plow and looks back is fit for the kingdom of God." The plow is a direct reference to that of Elisha.

While the rebuffed willing follower reflects the final moments of Elijah's interaction with Elisha, the followers asking for a delay recall their initial encounter in 1 Kings 19:19–21 (see above §, Calling Disciples: "Follow me"). Unless it is read against the background of Elijah's initial and final moments with Elisha, Yeshua's attitude, which both calls some unprepared disciples and rejects willing ones, appears arbitrary. Why Elijah asks Elisha to leave him alone remains a puzzle, a puzzle no Gospel explains. The Gospels take the puzzle as it is and apply it to Yeshua.

Ascension

Though Hebrews 11 only remembers Enoch as one who did not experience death, Elijah's rapture by chariots of fire (2 Kgs 2:11) is reflected in two Gospels as Yeshua's ascension to heaven after having transmitted his final recommendations to his disciples (Mark 16:19; Luke 24:51). In this particular case, the evangelists were more selective. Yeshua needs no chariots to take him to the right hand of God. Though the horse is the most mentioned animal in the Bible, even more than the lion and the ass, horses are connoted negatively. For biblical writers, horses are warhorses. They represent invading armies (Jer 8:6). As such, they embody the arrogance of the godless who trust in their own power (Pss 33:17; 147:10). Therefore, Yeshua enters Jerusalem on a colt and ascends to heaven without a chariot.

Staves and Healings

Modeling Yeshua on Elijah and Elisha did not entail wooden reproduction. Whereas Mark 6:8 has Yeshua allow his disciples to take only a staff when they go on mission, Matthew 10:10 and Luke 9:3 forbid them to take even a staff. To show that Yeshua is the new Elisha, Mark borrowed the staff Elisha gave to his servant Gehazi as a token of his might at the bedside of the son of the Shunammite woman. Once Mark had made the point, Matthew and Luke could raise Yeshua above Elisha by endowing the disciples with their master's powers without any material sign of it.

To make sure his readers picked up the point, Luke added a weird command. Yeshua forbids his seventy disciples to greet anyone on their way (Luke 10:4), another echo of Elisha's sending of Gehazi, urging him to hurry toward the dead child (2 Kgs 4:29).

Matthew signaled Yeshua's connection with Elisha differently. Instead of a prohibition to greet anyone on the way, Matthew 17:16 has some disciples incapable of healing an epileptic. Again, Gehazi is the model, as he was unable to revive the son of the Shunammite (2 Kgs 4:31). To underline the point, Matthew 17 mentions Elijah five times (verses 3, 4, 10, 11, and 12), insisting in verse 12 that Elijah has already come, though the previous verse states the contrary. Putting himself in Elisha's sandals by healing the epileptic whom the disciples were unable to heal implies that since Elijah has already come, Yeshua is Elisha, Elijah's successor.

Yeshua's status as the heir and successor of Elijah and Elisha is reflected in the way the books of the Old Testament are ordered in Christian Bible. Whereas Hebrew and Jewish Bibles end with 2 Chronicles, Christian Bibles end with Malachi 4:4–6:

> Lo, I will send *you the prophet Elijah* before the great and terrible day of the LORD comes. He will turn the hearts of parents to their children and the hearts of children to their parents, so that I will not come and strike the land with a curse.

As discussed above in relation to the transfiguration, the Christian canonical sequence illustrates the notion of progressive revelation. The Gospels following immediately after Malachi demonstrate that Yeshua is greater then Moses (the Law) as well as greater than Elijah (the Prophets).

A Carpet of Cloaks for the New King

As much as the healing of King Jeroboam's hand in 1 Kings 13:6 is echoed in the Synoptic Gospels, though it is set before the arrival of Elijah on the scene (Table 1), the evangelists borrowed another motif, this time after the end of the Elijah-Elisha cycle, to illustrate the proclamation of Yeshua's kingship. Upon hearing that Elisha's envoy anointed Jehu, his fellow officers "hurriedly took their cloaks and spread them for him on the bare steps; and they blew the trumpet, and proclaimed, "Jehu is king" (2 Kgs 9:13).

No trumpet is blown when Yeshua enters Jerusalem on a colt. Instead it is the hosannas shouted by his followers that trumpet the arrival of the new king and set the city in turmoil (Matt 21:10). Though the leafy branches in Mark 11:8 and Matthew 21:8 eventually inspired the name of Palm Sunday, Luke 19:36 ignores those branches. Luke chose to stay closer to the episode of the acclamation of Jehu by only having the crowd spread cloaks (the Septuagint and the Gospels use the same word, ἱμάτιον) for Yeshua's passage.

Luke also integrated Yeshua's weeping over the city (Luke 19:41) in his own elaboration of Mark's version of Palm Sunday. This time, Luke is not alluding to the anointment of Jehu, but to Hazael's, the King of Damascus, who sat on the throne after murdering Bar Hadad at the instigation of Elisha (2 Kgs 8:11–15). Elisha wept when he realized what anointing Hazael would mean for Israel. The God of Israel was raising Hazael on the Damascus throne to punish his people Israel for its unfaithfulness. The punishment would entail setting Israel's fortresses on fire, killing their young men with the sword, dashing in pieces their little ones, and ripping up their pregnant women (2 Kgs 8:12; 10–13).

Remembered as the echo of Elisha's own tears, Yeshua's weeping over Jerusalem takes on a deeper meaning. Though the Gospels avoid the military feats of Elijah and Elisha, Luke overturned Hazael's. The upcoming destruction motivates both Elisha's and Yeshua's tears (in both cases, the verb, κλαίω), but instead of being the instrument of the divine punishment as Hazael was, Yeshua is about to take upon himself Israel's guilt and die as a sacrificial lamb of the Passover.

Conclusion: New Light from the Old Testament on the New Testament

The above examples are but a selection of the many cases of appropriation of themes from the Elijah-Elisha cycle for the portrayal of Yeshua in the Gospels. There are certainly more to be identified. Though Christians have long read the Old Testament in light of the New Testament, it is worth the effort of doing the opposite. Reading the New Testament in light of the Old reveals the exegetical work accomplished by each evangelist. It throws light on points that otherwise remain hidden when their origin is not traced in the Hebrew Scriptures. Details like Zebedee remaining in the boat with the hired men are loose ends until they are seen as reflections of Elisha's parents and plowmen whom he fed with the flesh of his oxen. That the sons of Zebedee do not even kiss their father underlines the urgency of Yeshua's call. Elijah had let Elisha return to kiss his parents, but Yeshua proffered chilling words instead: "Let the dead bury the dead!" Elisha's farewell meal opens insights for the discerning reader aware of the interplay between the calls of Elisha and that of Yeshua. The main point of Elisha's meal offered to the plowmen is there is no turning back. Boiling the oxen with the wood of the equipment, Elisha graphically burned his bridges. By contrast, Yeshua himself, rather than his disciples, fed others and rejected his own family, a warning for those following Yeshua on the narrow path.

Walking in the steps of the Gospel writers, Bible readers are invited to interpret the New Testament in light of the Old as much as the Old in light of the New. Recognizing that the Gospel writers used the Hebrew Scriptures as the template for their depictions of Yeshua in no way downplays the importance of the New Testament. Taking this point seriously is to imitate Christ and his disciples by pondering the entire Scriptures, following their steps in weaving biblical motifs, using parallels and contrasts in creative ways for living and teaching Yeshua's message.

4

Yeshua as Master
in Biblical Argumentation

IN THE FIRST CHAPTER of the Gospel of Mark, Yeshua's audience is awestruck by the power of his teaching: "They were all amazed, and they kept on asking one another, "What is this? A new teaching—with authority!" (Mark 1:27)

Besides the signs and wonders discussed above (chapter 3), the Gospels have numerous episodes in which Yeshua is engaged in theological arguments with different Jewish theologians, arguments which invariably display his ability to turn the tables on his opponents.

This chapter focuses upon some of these theological disputes to show how Yeshua uses the Hebrew Scriptures to make his points.

CONDEMNING THE DEVIL
WITH PSALM 91

The Synoptic Gospels introduce Yeshua's career with a theological contest with the most formidable opponent ever: the devil himself. The very notion of temptation in the wilderness may be an echo of Elijah's own temptation to give up hope when he fled from Jezebel (1 Kgs 19). At first, an angel revived him with freshly baked bread and water. Then, Elijah encountered a mighty wind, an earthquake, a fire, and finally, a soft murmur that reaffirmed his mission.

Contrary to Mark 1:12–13, Matthew and Luke present a detailed scriptural contest in the wilderness (Matt 4:1–11; Luke 4:1–13). The three rounds in which Yeshua tackles the devil loosely follow the sequence of 1 Kings 19: bread, testing, and idolatry.

Satan opens fire with a challenge "If you are the Son of God, command this stone to become a loaf of bread." Besides the obvious temptation after forty days of fasting, the invitation is an inference from the Exodus story of manna by which God fed his children in the wilderness, and even more clearly an allusion to the angel that brought a cake baked on hot stones to Elijah (1 Kgs 19:6).

Yeshua's reply carefully dodges the tricky Son of Man issue by stating that humans "do not live on bread alone," a truncated quote of Deuteronomy 8:3. Yet, this focus on Yeshua's human nature does not imply that he is not the Son of God. With his question, the devil himself acknowledges at least the possibility that Yeshua is God's cherished son, in agreement with the voice from heaven heard when Yeshua was baptized (Matt 3:17; Mark 1:11; Luke 3:22) thus making it very difficult for any human to contest it. Hence, the first round ends with an affirmation of Yeshua's double nature, being both divine and human.

The second (Luke) and third round (Matthew) focus on political authority. Satan may allude to Job 2:6 where God delivers Job into the power of the devil. Nowhere in the book of Job is it written that God later withdrew Job from the devil's power. Hence, generalizing his ongoing dominion over Job to every kingdom of the world, the tempter claims that he is free to offer power and glory to anyone he wishes (Matt 4:9; Luke 4:6). Were Yeshua to bow down and worship the devil, all this glory would be his.

Yeshua strikes back with quotes from Deuteronomy 6:13 and 10:20 that forbid idolatry: "Worship the Lord your God, and serve only him." Yeshua thus sidesteps the issue implied by his opponent's claim of world dominion, that every ruler has received his power from the evil one, and not from God.

Then the devil places Yeshua on the pinnacle of the Jerusalem temple, saying "If you are the Son of God, throw yourself down from here." To justify this challenge, the devil tries a literal approach to the biblical text with a quoting from Psalm 91:11–12: "For it is written, 'He will command his angels concerning you, to protect you,' and 'On their hands they will bear you up, so that you will not dash your foot against a stone.'"

Against such a straightforward biblical quote, Yeshua retorts with another quote that combines scriptural elements from Deuteronomy and Isaiah: "Do not put the Lord your God to the test." This precept alludes to the rebellious episode at Massah that is recalled in Deuteronomy 6:16. Though the proverbial poison is to be found in the tail of a discourse, in this instance it is in the preceding verse addressed as a warning to the Israelites. Transposed in the contest, it works as a scathing condemnation of Yeshua's opponent: "because the LORD your God, who is present with you, is a jealous God, the anger of the LORD your God is kindled against you and he will destroy you from the face of the earth" (Deut 6:15). Though that part is not quoted, all readers versed in Scripture would pick up the points. First, the words "the Lord is present with you" claim that God stands beside the devil, thus reaffirming Yeshua's own divine status. Second, Yeshua declares that God is angry with the devil and that he shall be destroyed.

The other scriptural allusion is to King Ahaz's refusal to ask for a sign (Isaiah 7:12). This time, the punchline is found in what follows, the famous oracle in verse 13: "the virgin shall be with child and bear a son, and you shall name him Immanuel." Again, a discerning reader conversant with Scripture would not be content with the actual quoted words. Knowing large portions of his Bible by heart, he or she obtains a deeper meaning by taking into account the larger context of the Old Testament passages from which the quotes are extracted.

READING FROM THE ISAIAH SCROLL AT NAZARETH

After this clash of theological giants, Yeshua finds himself in his hometown on a Sabbath day. Yeshua enters a synagogue at Nazareth where he is handed a scroll to read aloud a passage from Isaiah:

> He unrolled the scroll and found the place where it was written: "The Spirit of the Lord is upon me, because he has anointed me to bring good news to the poor. He has sent me to proclaim release to the captives and recovery of sight to the

> blind, to let the oppressed go free, to proclaim
> the year of the Lord's favor." (Luke 4:17–19)

Yeshua then hands back the scroll. As everyone present knows him as Joseph's son, they stare at him, so Yeshua adds: "Today this scripture has been fulfilled in your hearing" (Luke 4:16–21). Yeshua openly claims to be the one whom Isaiah spoke about and that in him the Prophets are fulfilled. How Yeshua happened to read that portion of Isaiah 61 is not told.

There are several ways to understand the choice of that passage. In light of later practice, this portion of Isaiah may have been the one set to be read on that particular Sabbath according to the synagogue lectionary. The miracle is that the synagogue attendant happened to ask Yeshua to read it. We have, however, no indication that such a set order of reading of prophetic texts existed already in the days of Yeshua or Luke. If not, either Yeshua searched for that passage on purpose, or he unrolled the scroll at random. The Greek verb used to convey that Yeshua "found the place where it was written" can equally mean that he searched for that passage or that he came upon it accidentally without seeking it.

There is no way to decide between these three options. Luke's point is to show that God had preordained what would be read by Yeshua the day he was asked to read in the synagogue. In any case, Providence guided both the choice of Isaiah 61:1–2 and the choice of Yeshua as its reader.

Religious authorities have always frowned upon bibliomancy—the random choice of a verse from a sacred book to answer a particular query. Christian history is full of stories of conversion by the chance hearing of biblical verses. For instance, it was upon hearing Matthew 19:21 read as he entered a church that Saint Antony decided to sell everything he had inherited. Saint Augustine converted upon hearing children sing *tolle lege*. *Tolle* in Latin is an invitation to throw lots to obtain an oracle by reading (*lege*) that oracle in a verse designated by the lots. According to his own account of the episode, the great Augustine took the children's song as a divine command to open the sacred book and read the first passage he would find. Seizing the book, his eyes first fell on Romans 13:14–15, which he took personally as the denunciation of his own loose living and a solemn call to conversion.[1]

The astonishment of the congregation as Yeshua sat down after handing back the Isaiah scroll is all the more justified if the passage he read was neither set in advance nor carefully searched for. Without the awareness of the importance of bibliomancy, modern readers miss the gist of what happened in the Nazareth synagogue on that Sabbath day. Luke wanted to show that it was God the Father rather than Yeshua himself who chose that text. As a case of bibliomancy, Yeshua, as much as the Nazareth assembly, found out the implications of the message transmitted by the Holy Spirit when John baptized Yeshua at the Jordan: "You are my Son, the beloved; with you I am well pleased" (Luke 3:22). Here, "my son" refers to the Messiah and "my beloved" refers to the Suffering Servant of Isaiah 52–53. In the unique Nazareth scene, Luke introduces the motif of the Suffering Servant in order to reject views that might equate Yeshua with Abraham, Moses, or Elijah. God himself selects a passage from Isaiah's suffering servant, which echoes God's own endearing words in the baptism scene, to insist that Yeshua is more than Elijah returned.

Being the Beloved with whom the Father is well pleased meant to bring good news to the poor, to release captives, to heal the blind, and to relieve the oppressed—all

---

1. Augustine, *Confessions of St. Augustine*, 8.12.27–28.

miracles Elijah and Elisha never performed. Yeshua puts these words into action the moment he escapes from Nazareth and reaches Capernaum where he performs his first healing (Luke 4:31–41). Rather than having the Son know everything right from the start, Yeshua discovers in stages the substance of his ministry. The process of ongoing revelation is reflected in the canonical order of Christian Bible, specifically the Malachi–Matthew sequence. Gospel readers experience this progression as they discover new practical implications of their faith as they progress along their own life cycle.

ONE WITH THE FATHER (JOHN 10)

While disputing in the Jerusalem Temple with some Jews, Yeshua equates himself with God in explicit terms by stating that "The Father and I are one" (John 10:30), angering the opponents of Yeshua to the point where they want to kill him (v. 31). Accused of blasphemy, Yeshua retorts: "Is it not written in your law, 'I said, you are gods'?" A superficial reading is unlikely to catch the force of Yeshua's point, even if a footnote informs the reader that Yeshua is quoting Psalm 82:6. Psalm 82 might in fact further confuse the reader who expects the Bible to reflect modern concepts of monotheism. To understand how Yeshua won that argument, the substance of the Psalm must be exposed with an eye to the Greek text as English translations tend to shy away from the apparent polytheism which transpires in that Psalm.

Psalm 82 is set in the context of the divine council, a kind of executive board holding regular meetings to administer worldly and heavenly affairs. Job 1–2 make readers privy to two such board meetings which discussed

Job's case. Psalm 82 offers another glimpse of a particularly heated session of the divine council. The agenda this time focuses entirely on internal affairs. Elohim, the chairman of the council, is furious with his colleagues and vents his anger by accusing them of professional incompetence. They judge unjustly and show partiality to the wicked when, in fact, they should give justice to the weak, protect the right of the lowly, and deliver them from the hand of the wicked. The situation is so bad that the foundations of the world are shaken. Fostering inequity instead of justice, these gods demonstrate their ignorance and their blindness, marks of the human condition which are unfit for gods. Hence the verdict pronounced by the head of the divine council: "I had declared you gods and children of the Most High, all of you, but as humans you shall die" (Ps 82:6–7). Having condemned his divine colleagues to death, God finds himself alone. The apparent polytheism of that Psalm is in fact an affirmation of monotheism.

The Jews rightly equate Yeshua's claim to be one with the Father with blasphemy and decide to stone him. Yeshua first asks for which of his good works are they condemning him to death? The Jews reply that he is condemned for making himself God, not for performing good works. Having made his opponents indirectly admit that he has done good works, Yeshua only need to quote the beginning of Elohim's verdict in Psalm 82:6: "I had declared you gods." Instead of citing the rest of the passage, he turns the Psalm upside down. Because Scripture cannot be annulled (John 10:35), the fact that there are more gods than one remains forever true. Because the gods of Psalm 82 were condemned to death for failing to deliver justice, he whom the Jews just admitted did good works cannot be accused of blasphemy, because his acts prove his divine status. The monotheism that arose after the elimination of the wicked gods of Psalm 82 was thus a temporary situation. Having rescued the weak and delivered them from the hand of the wicked, Yeshua cannot be accused of blasphemy since his works qualify him for divine status. Yeshua closes his plea with an invitation to believe at least his works if his opponents cannot accept his divine status. This is ironical since it is these works, Yeshua argues, that prove his divinity. Instead of stating that Yeshua and the Father are two elements of a trinity, John simply states that the Father is in Yeshua and that Yeshua is in the Father (John 10:38).

A CRYPTIC MESSAGE FOR JOHN THE BAPTIST (LUKE 7)

According to Matthew 14:2, Herod imprisoned John the Baptist for criticizing his marriage with Herodias, his brother's ex-wife. Yeshua's fame as a great prophet reaches the baptist in jail, and he sends two of his disciples to Yeshua. The question put to Yeshua is "Are you the one who is to come, or are we to wait for another?" (Matt 11:3; Luke 7:19–20). In real life, John would have been concerned about his own fate. He would have tried to figure out the implications of Yeshua's ministry for his own situation as a prisoner. As Yeshua and John the Baptist are related through their mothers (see Luke 1:36), one would expect Yeshua to be supportive of his cousin. Enough clues are found in the Gospels to suspect that there was, however, much rivalry between the first followers of Yeshua and those of the baptist. The strongest affirmation of Yeshua's primacy is found in John 1, a long chapter in which John himself is made to declare that his followers must follow Yeshua.

The Synoptic Gospels are hardly less graphic about John's subordination to Yeshua. In Mark 1:7, the baptist is made to proclaim that he is not worthy to stoop down and untie the thong of Yeshua's sandals. As in the Nazareth scene discussed above, Luke focuses on the figure of the suffering servant. In answer to the question of whether or not he is the one who is to come, Yeshua tells John's messengers to report what they saw and heard: "the blind receive their sight, the lame walk, the lepers are cleansed, the deaf hear, the dead are raised, the poor have good news brought to them" (Luke 7:22; see also Isaiah 26:9, 29:18–19, 35:5–6, 61:1).

These mighty acts were certainly good news for those who benefited from them, but did they answer John's query? The Greek words for "the coming one" recall Psalm 118:26: "Blessed is the one who comes in the name of the LORD." That Yeshua was the blessed one would hardly have direct implications on John's fate. That he was indeed the awaited Messiah would have given hope to the baptist in jail if, for instance, Zechariah 9:11–12 had been quoted. These verses state that the coming Messiah will set prisoners free from the waterless pit.

The punch line here is in what is *not* said. For anyone conversant with messianic texts in the Hebrew Scriptures, Zechariah would have been the passage relevant to John's situation. The fact that Yeshua did not quote such a passage is highly significant. It tells the readers that John the Baptist is to die in prison in circumstances related in Mark 6 and Matthew 14. Luke simply has Herod state that he beheaded John (Luke 8:9). Instead of describing the banquet that led to John's murder, Luke 7 has Yeshua wait until John's envoys are gone to explain that the baptist is more than a prophet, that none among those born of women is greater than John, and yet, "the least in the kingdom of God is greater than he" (Luke 7:26–27).

That John is greater than a prophet would be bitter-sweet consolation to John and to his disciples. John's superiority dismisses the entire Old Testament and sets John and his disciples in between testaments, only to dismiss them too with the next saying. Any of Yeshua's followers is greater than John and any of those who insist on following John rather than Yeshua. The concluding verse reveals the intensity of the rivalry between the two groups: "And blessed is anyone who takes no offense at me" (Luke 7:23). This is an indirect curse to anyone who takes offense at the superiority of Yeshua over John.

Overfamiliarity with superficial readings of the gospel tends to cloud the theological debates reflected in the New Testament with a haze of soft love. In fact, the harshness of these debates reflects real-life struggles that were no less sharp than those read in the supposedly more violent Old Testament.

YESHUA TOPPLES THE GOLDEN CALF AND SIGNS HIS OWN DEATH WARRANT

No less harsh is the scene of Yeshua's cleansing of the temple. It must have been understood as crucial to Yeshua's portrayal, since all four Gospels transmit it. Yeshua drove out those who were selling sacrificial victims in the temple (Luke 19:45), overturning the tables of the money changers and the seats of the pigeon sellers (Matt 21:12; Mark 11:15). John 2:13–15 adds oxen and sheep to the list of clutter in the temple precincts, and puts a whip of cords in Yeshua's hand for increased effect.

The Synoptic Gospels conclude the episode with a modified quote from Jeremiah 7:11: "Has this house which is called by my name become a den of robbers in your sight?" In the mouth of Yeshua, the quote becomes: "My house shall be called a house of prayer, but you are making it a den of robbers." Obviously, the change from Jeremiah's "this house" to "my house" would be blasphemous in the eyes of the religious authorities who would understand it as a claim to divine status. But there is more.

Immediately following the image of the den of robbers, Jeremiah's sermon at the temple gate reminds the audience about the fate of the temple at Shiloh, where the name of the Lord dwelt until God himself destroyed it in punishment for Israel's wickedness. The sting of Yeshua's words is found not so much in the actual verse he quotes, but in the next verse, which warns the people of Jerusalem that their temple will suffer the same fate if they do not mend their ways. Once again, one has to consider the context of the quote to attain the deeper meaning of the scene.

For the evangelists, Yeshua's point is crystal clear and the temple authorities immediately start looking for ways to have Yeshua executed (Mark 11:18; Luke 19:47). The temple was not only the religious and cultural center of the region; it was the source of revenues of the priests and scribes. An attack on the thriving temple economy was tantamount to an attack on their existence.

ARGUING TO THE VERY END (PSALM 22)

Hanging on the cross and about give up the ghost, Yeshua utters the famous agonizing words, "My God, my God, why have you forsaken me" (Matt 27:46; Mark 15:34)? Though Yeshua was undoubtedly suffering the excruciating fate of all crucified, the Gospels do not make a show of these death throes. Instead, that scene becomes the grand finale that reveals to all what Yeshua had proclaimed during his ministry: that he came to fulfill Scripture.

As is well known, the question "Why have you forsaken me?" is a quote from Psalm 22. It is the only one of the last seven utterances of Yeshua on the cross to appear in more than one Gospel (Matt 27:46; Mark 15:34). From a theological standpoint, Yeshua had to be abandoned by God for atonement to take place, but these words are no mere cries of despair as if, faced by death, the Son suddenly lost faith in the Father.

Besides the introductory question Yeshua quotes on the cross, Psalm 22 has clearly inspired the scene of the Roman soldiers dividing Yeshua's clothes in John 19:23–24: "For dogs are all around me; a company of evildoers encircles me. My hands and feet have shriveled; I can count all my bones. They stare and gloat over me; they divide my clothes among themselves, and for my clothing they cast lots" (Ps 22:16–18).

Mark and Matthew elaborate a subtle argumentation that requires a thorough knowledge of the entire psalm. Psalm 22:4–6 has David comparing himself to his ancestors: "In you our ancestors trusted; they trusted, and you delivered them. To you they cried, and were saved; in you they trusted, and were not put to shame. But I am a worm, and not human; scorned by others, and despised by the people." Whereas the Israelites of old were systematically saved whenever they cried out to God, David sets himself in a separate category. To achieve a deep rhetorical effect, he deprecates himself as being a worm, not a human, probably in the hope to spur God to rescue him. Then, David quotes the words of mockers who challenge him to "Commit your cause to the LORD; let him deliver—let him rescue the one in whom he delights!" (Ps 22:8). Yeshua's quote of the first line of Psalm 22 would inevitably evoke the rest of the psalm in the mind of any one who had memorized many such psalms and could recite them effortlessly. In this context, the taunt "the one in whom he delights" is turned into a claim of Yeshua's divinity, an echo of the divine words heard at the Jordan when Yeshua received the Holy Spirit (see above). Moreover, Yeshua's divine status is reinforced by the last phrase of Psalm 22:10: "Since my mother bore me you have been my God."

To modern eyes, the identification of Yeshua with the psalmist is rather convoluted as it selects a few fragments, ignoring the overall context of the psalm. This is precisely what today's exegetes are taught *not* to do. Yet, the evangelists employ the techniques of biblical exegesis current in their days. Matthew and Mark mine Psalm 22 for material to mark the climax of Yeshua's ministry on the cross. With much irony, in Mark it is the Roman centurion who recognizes that Yeshua was the son of God (Mark 15:39), putting to shame those versed in the Hebrew Scriptures.

STEPHEN'S MARTYRDOM (ACTS 7)

Beyond the Gospels, Acts 7 portrays Stephen as the first Christian martyr. Accused of repeated slander against the temple, Stephen is interrogated by the Jewish ruling council. As a worthy follower of Yeshua, Stephen pronounces a long speech in which he reminds his audience that the idea to replace the wilderness tabernacle with a temple was David's, but it was only Solomon who actually built it (Acts 7:46–47). The implication is that if the tabernacle made according to the blueprint supplied by God had been good enough until then, why could it not be good enough afterward, since "the Most High does not dwell in houses made with human hands" (Acts 7:48)? Surely, the temple made after the desires of a human, even a king, is no match for the tabernacle made after God's model. Hence, Stephen adds a quote from Isaiah: "Heaven is my throne, and the earth is my footstool. What kind of house will you build for me, says the Lord, or what is the place of my rest" (Isa 66:1; Acts 7:48–49)?

The full bearings of the polemic is found not in the actual quoted words, but in the verses that follow, in this case the Greek version of Isaiah 66:3:

> But the lawless who sacrifices to me a calf is like one who kills a dog, and he who offers fine flour, like swine's blood; he who has given frankincense for a memorial, like a blasphemer. And these have chosen their own ways and their abominations, which their soul wanted. (New English Translation of the Septuagint)

Equating the sacrifice of a calf with that of a dog, and the offering of flour with swine's blood would have been highly offensive to Jews for whom these sacrifices were pre-scribed by Moses. Stephen's critique of the sacrificial econ-omy is as scathing as Yeshua's cleansing of the temple and it uses the same method. The intended readers of the Gospels and Acts would have picked up the point and uncovered a deeper meaning than meets the eye when quotes are read in isolation from their larger context. Catching their presence requires a deep knowledge of the Hebrew Bible, which also displays the importance of this corpus of texts for Chris-tianity today. This sophisticated technique illustrates how Yeshua accomplished the Law and the Prophets. He did not do so superficially, by quoting verses here and there as is often done by fundamentalists today. His mastery in theological argumentation drew from the entire Hebrew Bible, an example for anyone wanting to extol Yeshua today.

Conclusion

To RECAP THE SUBSTANCE of the previous chapters, the co-opting and reworking of traditions and motifs is ubiquitous in the Gospels, as it was in antiquity and still is today, in particular in matters pertaining to faith. Chapter 1 argues that the portrayal of Yeshua in the New Testament is based on a mirror effect with the concept of *imago Dei*. As Genesis 1 states that God created humans in his image, the divinity of Yeshua is expressed by mirroring paradigmatic figures from the Hebrew Bible, mostly Elijah and Elisha, but also Moses, Isaiah, and Jeremiah. These figures were crucial to demonstrate how Yeshua fulfilled expectations. But the evangelists, each in his own way, also made use of the templates provided by the Torah, the books of Kings, and the Prophets, to counter expectations current among their audience.

Today, we stand at a turning point. For many centuries, Christians were taught to read the Old Testament in light of the New Testament. The result is that many Christians consider that they do not need to bother with the Old Testament. A similar situation pertains in academic circles. Due to increasing specialization, New Testament exegetes rarely have the familiarity with the Old Testament that is necessary to pick up the allusions to the Old Testament and recover how the evangelist used them to weave them into a new tapestry.[1]

The main thrust of this work is to show that reading the New Testament in light of the Old, and in light of its ancient Near Eastern context, is following the steps of the evangelists who lived in the Near East and for whom the Old Testament was *the* Bible. Cut flowers make beautiful but ephemeral bouquets, because they have been severed from their roots.

Besides the towering figures of the Hebrew Bible, the great mythological figures of the ancient Levant were co-opted to place Yeshua on a level higher than any human figure portrayed in the Old Testament. Hence, chapter 2 shows how the ancient motif of a deity conquering chaos was first appropriated for the Israelite god, and later reworked and applied to Yeshua. When he calmed the storm and trod on the menacing waters, Yeshua acted as the biblical Creator who acted in this instance in the same way as the storm god Baal.

Chapter 3 shows that Yeshua's miracles reproduce most of those performed by Elijah and Elisha. The Elijah-Elisha template reveals what the evangelists left out, which in turn allows one to pinpoint what was considered inappropriate for Yeshua. While the military feats of Elijah and Elisha are not repeated in the Gospels, a dozen key episodes in Yeshua's life are clearly modeled after the prophetic careers of Elijah and Elisha to portray Yeshua as prophet.

Chapter 4 reviews the numerous disputes in which Yeshua is involved with various opponents. Yeshua is presented as the ultimate master in theological argumentation. His command of the Hebrew Bible allows him to rebuff the sharpest attacks as he uses the same techniques as his

1. A recent exception is Tarazi, *Rise of Scripture.*

adversaries to make his point and offer new understandings of traditional texts that reflect the needs of Christian communities.

All in all, it took a plethora of images, literary techniques, and figures to explain who this first-century rabbi was. From a faith perspective, our feeble words never can do justice to the divine. Yeshua's disciples, as much as we modern readers of the Gospels, are confronted with the question Yeshua asked at Caesarea Philippi: "Who do *you* say that I am" (Matt 16:15; Mark 8:29)? This question is the turning point in Yeshua's career in the different Gospels. From then on, Yeshua turns all his attention toward Jerusalem and prepares for his passion. Peter, the first pope, is praised for his right answer as he explains: "You are the Christ (Messiah), the Son of the Living God" (Matt 16:16; Mark 8:29). Peter's answer extols Yeshua; another answer would not do justice to the testimony of the Christian Scriptures and the tradition of the church.

Besides the theological point of Yeshua's identity as the Messiah, the Gospels identified the Messiah as the suffering servant, a point contested ever since by Jews and Muslims. At a time when the number of humans massacred in the name of God is again on the rise, it is not vain to remind ourselves that Yeshua—whether as rabbi, Son of God or great prophet—is the son of the Living God who chose to suffer for the world and who rejected the military deeds of Elijah and Elisha. Upon this point the three main monotheisms can agree.

Doctrinal disagreements will remain, but agreeing that Yeshua is the son of the Living God can save lives. Different perspectives on the identity of Yeshua are inherent not only in the three monotheisms, but already in the New Testament. To signify what his work means for humanity, the evangelists gathered pieces collected from all available sources and rearranged them into a new mosaic. That the resulting mosaic is not one, but four Gospels—though there were quite a few more before these four were canonized— shows that the process of accumulation and composition can never produce *the* single and final whole. The churches wisely resisted the temptation to produce the definitive gospel. Harmonized versions of the different Gospels were not well received. The churches equally resisted the temptation to produce a gospel purged of Old Testament references such as Marcion's, or a gospel free of mythological and miraculous elements like a modern *Lives of Jesus*.[2] The ability to resist these temptations springs from a deep awareness of the nature of tradition, as the result of the incarnation.

INCARNATION AND TRADITION

Incarnation, the flesh-and-blood expression of God in the humanity of Yeshua, is the cornerstone of Christianity. The appropriation of pagan myths, Hebrew figures, and Jewish argumentation methods discussed in the previous chapters is the outcome of the theological concept of incarnation in the realm of the production of sacred texts.

In practical terms, incarnation fosters the formation of a religious tradition rooted in previous cultural traditions, a religious tradition that claims to be new because it presents itself as the legitimate heir to the best achievements of previous generations. Rather than pretending that it fell from the sky free from any human mediation, Christianity presents itself as the next link in a long chain of religious traditions. The Word Incarnate came as a man, a first-century Jew, very much in the same way as the Hebrew

2. Lieu, *Marcion and the Making*.

Scriptures, today the main part of the Christian Bibles, was produced in one of the most peripheral regions of the ancient Empires that ruled the Levant, Judea/Yehud.

THE FUTURE OF TRADITION

By definition, God is beyond time and thus not subject to change. Nevertheless, human understandings of God are not imbued with eternal validity. The ancient Sumerians, Hittites, Babylonians, and Egyptians invested huge efforts in monumental and literary expressions of their religions. Some of the temples they built, some of the texts they wrote, are still accessible to us thanks to archaeology. Yet, as religious expressions, they passed. Judaism, followed by Christianity and Islam, declared the great religions of the Levant pagan and supplanted them. The priests of Marduk and of Ra probably believed that their religion was eternal, but it died, and there is no reason to think that Judaism, Christianity, and Islam are immune from such a fate. Supercessionist claims are already made by the Baha'i and the Druze, for example.

The future of any tradition, religious or otherwise, rests on its ability to maintain a double allegiance: faithfulness to its roots (the past) and relevance to the host cultures (the present). The Gospels achieved relevance by drawing upon Jewish and pagan elements, appropriating and reworking what was considered worthy of attention. At two millennia, Christianity has reached a respectable age. Like its two monotheistic siblings, it has weathered many crises.

The universalism inherent to the three monotheisms certainly contributed to their historical successes. Universalism ensured that a particular religion was not tied to a particular culture. In this sense, universalism was a token of stability in the midst of political upheavals. But at the same time, the disconnection of religious expressions from particular cultural expressions can foster the illusion that religion is also disconnected from temporal contingencies.

If the God of yesterday is the same as the God of today, he is also the same as the God of tomorrow. But human understandings and perceptions of an immutable God change constantly because religion is incarnation. Hence, our present understanding can only be set above those of our ancestors in the sense that ours is more relevant for now, but this neither makes past understandings obsolete nor present understandings eternal. A living faith recognizes its roots, which fosters the growth of future branches that will not be identical to those of today's tree.

The contribution of the present study to Christianity's future resides in the three ingredients it presents: the pagan motifs (chapter 2), the Old Testament figures (chapter 3), and the use of Old Testament quotes (chapter 4). The New Testament combined these ingredients into a new whole. The success of the recipe depended much on the artful combination or appropriation of these ancient ingredients.

A tradition based on appropriation of older ingredients implies resisting the temptation that is particularly acute at the moment: the fundamentalist temptation. The pull towards fundamentalism is currently felt in all religions. Fundamentalism is a natural reaction to the erasure of boundaries effected by modern means of communication and by the erosion of nations. There are many advantages to being able to travel around the world or to communicate instantly with friends and business partners anywhere in the world. The backlash is that in the global world, one feels a little lost and needs a small village of friends who look, think, and feel like "me" despite the physical distance;

in other words, a community. The friends and likes of the social media are essential to foster that sense of belonging upon which to build identity, one's special character that makes "me" different from the masses. In many ways, religious fundamentalism contributes to this quest for identity and community, the desire to stand out from the crowd, to belong to a little flock of elect.

The fundamentalist temptation expresses itself as a fascination for a pure tradition that must be preserved from changes and from corruption from outside. This attitude is not exempt from a certain contempt for the world as God made it, an excessive belief in the power of evil over God's creation, and most of all, a narrowing of boundaries to foster a reassuring identity. In a world that has never changed so rapidly, it is only natural for believers to feel somewhat overwhelmed by the news and seek comfort in tradition. In the long run, however, the isolation of one's own small and reassuring group runs the risk of negating the very meaning of Catholicism—the universal validity of the Christian faith.

Because believers today face different challenges from the challenges believers of the first centuries faced, it is crucial to stand up to the challenges of the present in order to prepare for the future. Understanding the process by which the Gospel writers extolled Yeshua by drawing upon a variety of sources can show us the way.

Bibliography

Abusch, Tzvi. "Marduk." In *Dictionary of Deities and Demons in the Bible,* edited by Karel van der Toorn et al., 543–49. Leiden: Brill, 1999.

Allison, Dale C. *The New Moses: A Matthean Typology.* Minneapolis: Fortress, 1993.

Anderson, James. *Monotheism and Yahweh's Appropriation of Baal.* London: Bloomsbury, 2015.

Aurelius Augustine. *The Confessions of St. Augustine.* Translated by Edward Pusey. The Harvard Classics. New York: P.F. Collier & Son, 1909.

Brodie, Thomas L. *The Birthing of the New Testament: The Intertextual Developments of the New Testament Writings.* Sheffield, UK: Sheffield Phoenix, 2004.

———. *The Crucial Bridge.* Collegeville, MN: Liturgical, 2000.

———. "Luke's Use of the Elijah-Elisha Narrative." In *The Elijah-Elisha Narrative in the Composition of Luke,* edited by John S. Kloppenborg and Joseph Verheyden, 6–36. Library of New Testament Studies 493. London: Bloomsbury, 2014.

Brown, Raymond E. "Jesus and Elisha." *Perspective* 12 (1971) 86–104.

Caputo, John D. *Heidegger and Aquinas: An Essay on Overcoming Metaphysics.* New York: Fordam University Press, 1982.

Carey, Holly J., *Jesus' Cry from the Cross: Towards a First Century Understanding of the Intertextual Relationship between Psalm 22 and the Narrative of Mark's Gospel.* Library of New Testament Studies 398. London: Bloomsbury, 2009.

Colledge, Malcolm A. R. *The Art of Palmyra.* London: Thames & Hudson, 1976.

Edelman, Diana. "Exodus and Pesach/Massot as Evolving Social Memory." In *Remembering (and Forgetting) in Judah's Early*

    Second Temple Period, edited by Christoph Levin and Ehud Ben Zvi, 161–93. Forschungen zum Alten Testaments 85. Tübingen: Mohr Siebeck, 2012.

Emerton, John. A. "Leviathan and ltn: The Vocalization of the Ugaritic Word for the Dragon." *Vetus Testamentum* 32 (1982) 327–31.

Ghantous, Hadi, *The Elisha-Hazael Paradigm and the Kingdom of Israel.* Sheffield, UK: Acumen, 2013.

Guillaume, Philippe. "Miracles Miraculously Repeated: Gospel Miracles as Duplication of Elijah-Elisha's." *Biblische Notizen* 98 (1999) 21–23.

Hachlili, Rachel. *Ancient Jewish Art and Archaeology in the Diaspora.* Leiden: Brill, 1998.

Hallo, William W., and William Kelly Simpson. *The Ancient Near East: A History.* 2nd ed. Fort Worth, TX: Harcourt Brace, 1998.

John Paul II. *Crossing the Threshold of Hope.* New York: Alfred Knopf, 1995.

Konradt, Matthias. *Das Evangelium Nach Matthäus.* Göttingen: Vandenhoeck & Ruprecht, 2015.

Lambert, Wilfred G. "The Historical Development of the Mesopotamian Pantheon: A Study in Sophisticated Polytheism." In *Unity & Diversity: Essays in the History, Literature, and Religion of the Ancient Near East,* edited by Hans Goedicke and J. J. M. Roberts, 191–200. Baltimore: Johns Hopkins University Press, 1975.

Lieu, Judith M. *Marcion and the Making of a Heretic God and Scripture in the Second Century.* Cambridge: Cambridge University Press, 2015.

Moessner, David P. "Luke 9:1–50: Luke's Preview of the Journey of the Prophet like Moses of Deuteronomy." *Journal of Biblical Literature* 102 (1983) 565–606.

Na'aman, Nadav. "The Israelite-Judahite Struggle for the Patrimony of Ancient Israel." *Biblica* 91 (2010) 1–23.

Nicklas, Tobias. "'Let the Dead Bury their Own Dead' (Matt 8:22 par. Luke 9:60): A Commandment without Impact for Christian Ethos?" In *Biblical Ethics and Application,* edited by Ruben Zimmermann and Stephan Joubert, 75–90. Contexts and Norms of New Testament Ethics 9. Tübingen: Mohr Siebeck, 2017.

Pardee, Dennis. "The Ba'lu Myth." In *The Context of Scripture,* edited by William W. Hallo, 1:241–74. 3 vols. Leiden: Brill, 1997.

Puig i Tàrrech, Armand. "The Glory on the Mountain. The Episode of the Transfiguration of Jesus." *New Testament Studies* 58.2 (2012) 151–72.

Scholz, Daniel J. *Jesus in the Gospels and Acts: Introducing the New Testament*. Winona, MN: Anselm Academic, 2009.

Shupak, Nili. "'He Hath Subdued the Water Monster/Crocodile': God's Battle with the Sea in Egyptian Sources." *Ex Oriente Lux* 40 (2006–2007) 77–89.

Smith, Mark. *God in Translation: Deities in Cross-Cultural Discourse in the Biblical World*. Forschungen zum Alten Testament 57. Tübingen: Mohr Siebeck, 2008.

Tanabe, Katsumi. *Sculptures of Palmyra*. Tokyo: Ancient Orient Museum, 1986.

Tarazi, Paul Nadim. *The Rise of Scripture*. St. Paul, MN: OCABS, 2017.

www.ingramcontent.com/pod-product-compliance
Lightning Source LLC
Chambersburg PA
CBHW071109090426
42737CB00013B/2543